FREEDOM OF SPEECH

A TRUE BOOK®

by

Christin Ditchfield

Children's Press®
A Division of Scholastic Inc.

New York Toronto London Auckland Sydney
Mexico City New Delhi Hong Kong
Danbury, Connecticut

An anti-war protester

Reading Consultant
Jeanne Clidas, Ph.D.
*National Reading Consultant
and Professor of Reading,
SUNY Brockport*

Content Consultant
Jonathan Riehl, J.D.
*Graduate Instructor,
Communications Studies
University of North Carolina,
Chapel Hill*

Library of Congress Cataloging-in-Publication Data

Ditchfield, Christin.
  Freedom of speech / by Christin Ditchfield.
      p. cm. — (A true book)
  Summary: Describes what freedom of speech is, how and why it is
guaranteed in the United States, how it is expressed, what its limits
are, what censorship is, and what some of the surrounding debates are.
  ISBN 0-516-22798-X (lib. bdg.)   0-516-27909-2 (pbk.)
  1. Freedom of speech—United States—Juvenile literature.
[1. Freedom of speech.] I. Title. II. Series.
  KF4772.Z9D58 2004
  342.73'0853—dc21

                                                    2003005175

1 2 3 4 5 6 7 8 9 10 R 13 12 11 10 09 08 07 06 05 04

Contents

People protesting against the government cutting funds for education

What Did You Say?

Every day, in every language, people speak out about things that are important to them. They share their thoughts and ideas. They express opinions. They support causes they believe in. People celebrate things they love and appreciate. They complain about things they think should be changed.

Nelson Mandela was jailed for twenty-six years for protesting South Africa's policy of apartheid (separating blacks and whites). Here he is shown revisiting his jail cell years later.

Sometimes speaking out can be dangerous. In certain countries and at certain times in history, people have been punished for speaking their minds. They have been forced to pay fines or to serve time in jail. Some people have even been killed for daring to express their **political** opinions or religious beliefs. Their voices were silenced by those who disagreed with them.

The great thinker Socrates was sentenced to death by his countrymen in ancient Greece. They disliked the way he questioned their behavior and challenged their ideas. In the 1600s, Italian **astronomer** Galileo taught that the sun is

Italian astronomer Galileo (at right) was arrested for disagreeing with leaders who wrongly believed that Earth is the center of the universe.

the center of the universe. Leaders arrested him for spreading lies. They mistakenly believed that Earth is the center of the universe. John Peter Zenger lived in the American colonies in the 1700s. He was brought to trial for publishing a newspaper that criticized the British government that ruled the colonies.

Soon after the United States of America became a country, its leaders created a document called the Constitution. The Constitution lays out the rules for the American system of government. The leaders of the young country believed that individual freedom was one of the most important principles of government. They had fought a war to be free from the unfair government of Great Britain. They wanted to be sure that their new government would protect the rights and freedoms of its citizens.

At first, the Constitution did not specifically list all of these freedoms. This concerned many government officials. So new laws, called **amendments**, were added. The first ten amendments to the Constitution are known as the Bill of Rights. The

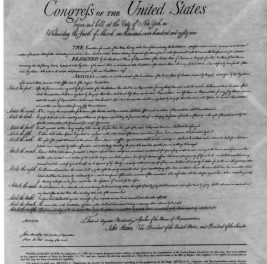

This painting (below) shows American leaders signing the United States Constitution. In September 1789, Congress proposed twelve amendments to the U.S. Constitution (left). Ten of these were adopted as the Bill of Rights.

First Amendment guarantees a number of freedoms, including freedom of speech.

Speaking Freely

Freedom of speech is the freedom to express ideas. It means that people can express their thoughts in conversations with friends and neighbors. They can make public speeches and take part in debates.

Freedom of speech also means freedom of the press—the right to express oneself in

Free speech allows people to openly disagree with each other about issues.

books, magazines, and newspapers. Freedom of speech protects opinions stated in music, movies, radio, and television. It even covers "speech acts"— when people show what they

think by wearing certain symbols, buttons, or armbands. Actions such as burning books or flags may also be considered a form of speech. In the United States, freedom of speech is guaranteed to all people, regardless of their age, race, education, religion, or ethnic background.

Freedom of speech means that U.S. citizens have the right to **criticize** their own government. They can organize protests to show their displeasure about

People demonstrating for the rights of people with disabilities

laws and policies they feel are unfair. They can march in parades, post signs, and pass out pamphlets. They can sign **petitions** demanding change. Neighbors can gather to discuss important issues that affect their community. They can object to things that they believe are harmful to others.

U.S. citizens can disagree with one another about moral issues—what is right and wrong. They can worship any

U.S. citizens have the right to sign petitions to change policies they believe are unfair.

way they choose, and they are free to share their religious faith with others.

Freedom of speech is powerful. By speaking up, people can draw attention to injustice.

17

Freedom of speech allows people to speak out about problems that need to be solved.

They can express concern for public health and safety. People can encourage and support those who cannot speak for themselves. They can introduce new ideas and work to bring about positive change in their own communities and in the country—and even in the world!

An anti-pollution rally in front of the Lincoln Memorial in Washington, D.C.

A Famous Speech

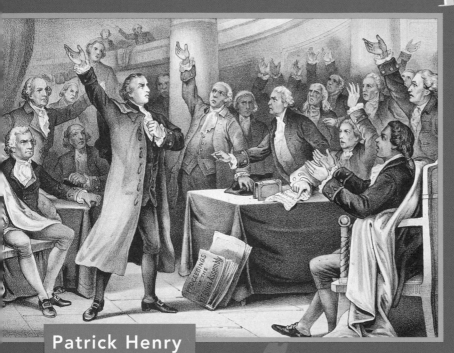

Patrick Henry

In the late 1700s, the people of the thirteen colonies in North America wanted to be free from the control of Great Britain. If colonists spoke out against the government, however, they could be arrested. They could lose their property or even their lives. In 1775, American leader Patrick Henry urged the colonists to be bold and courageous in their fight for freedom. Nothing was more important. "I know not what course others may take," he said, "but as for me, give me liberty or give me death!"

Speaking Responsibly

The First Amendment gives U.S. citizens the right to freedom of speech. It does not, however, give them the freedom to speak out at any time, in any place, in any way. There are limits. For instance, a community can require a group to get a **permit** to march in a parade or protest. Officials cannot refuse to grant a permit because they dislike the group's message. Officials *can* refuse to grant a permit if the demonstration will disrupt

The police may arrest demonstrators if they disrupt traffic or disturb businesses.

A student handing out a pamphlet from an environmental group

major traffic, threaten private property, or cause a public-safety risk. Because free speech is so important, it is very rare that a permit is not granted.

People who want to hand out pamphlets on private property must get permission from the

23

owner beforehand. Private property includes such places as business offices, restaurants, hotels, shops, and movie theaters.

People can choose to express themselves in ways that are **offensive** to others. They may say cruel and hateful things if they want to. Even if others disagree with their message, people have the right to make their voices heard. However, they may not use "fighting words" in public speeches. This means they cannot purposely say things meant to stir people to commit acts of violence against others. It is against the law to encourage people to commit crimes.

Although it is illegal to stir people to violence, freedom of speech does allow people to say things that others may find offensive.

During World War II, the government inspected mail to prevent messages that might aid the enemy from being sent overseas.

The government can keep certain information from being shared with the public if that information could put the nation's security at risk. For example, during a war, a newspaper cannot print the times troops will be moved from place to place. That might allow an enemy to learn important battle plans and possibly attack the soldiers.

There are also laws that require stores to keep certain movies, books, and other materials away from children. Though it is not

Some people have asked the government to put warning labels on music recordings containing language not suitable for children.

The **Parental Advisory** is a notice to parents that recordings identified by this logo may contain strong language

required by law, some television networks have agreed not to air certain programs with adult content during times when children are likely to tune in.

Laws keep people from using their freedom of speech to damage other people deliberately, but public figures such as movie stars or politicians are not protected from criticism. Still, it is a crime to damage or destroy a person's

reputation, business, or family life by spreading lies about him or her. When such lies are spoken, they are called slander. Written attacks are called libel. Those who engage in slander or libel may be taken to court and forced to pay fines. They may be required to make a public apology or print a **retraction** correcting the false information. American citizens must use their freedom of speech responsibly.

The Trouble with Censorship

When people discuss freedom of speech, they often debate the issue of censorship. Censorship is the attempt to prevent others from expressing their thoughts or ideas. Censorship may begin when an individual, group, or government decides that some form of speech is harmful to the public.

People demonstrating against censorship

Perhaps the expression is rude, shocking, or unpleasant. Perhaps it contains bad language. It may include sharp criticism of community leaders. It could mock a particular race or religion. The material may be unsuitable for

children and young adults. Sometimes, the ideas are just new and
different—and therefore might
cause fear among some people.
For whatever reason, if someone
attempts to stop the expression,
silence it, or remove the offensive
part, he or she has censored it.

In earlier times, governments
often arrested people who made
speeches criticizing their actions.
Newspapers and magazines
often would not print certain
stories because they feared
harsh reactions.

Book burning is a form of censorship. In 2001, a church group in New Mexico gathered to destroy books and games it found offensive.

Even recently in the United States, parents have requested that libraries remove some books from their shelves. Schools have refused to allow students to wear particular symbols or styles of dress associated with some sort of protest. Under pressure from the public, theaters have refused to show movies that some people might find offensive. These are all examples of censorship.

Some people claim that any attempt to limit free speech is censorship. They feel that just because people disagree with a message doesn't mean its speaker should be silenced. Others claim that some limits are necessary. They feel that ordinary

In 1965, some students sued their school after being suspended for wearing armbands to protest the Vietnam War. The U.S. Supreme Court ruled in their favor, saying that armbands were a form of expression protected by the First Amendment.

people have a right to be protected from people who abuse their freedom of speech or refuse to speak responsibly.

A Symbol that Speaks

By wearing or displaying **memorial** ribbons, people can show their support for a cause without saying a word. Certain colors represent certain concerns. Red ribbons are worn to raise awareness about AIDS, a deadly disease. Pink ribbons encourage support for women who have breast cancer. Yellow ribbons help people remember loved ones who are missing or far away from home. After the terrorist attacks on September 11, 2001, people began wearing ribbons in red, white, and blue—the colors of the United States flag.

Finding a Balance

People have long struggled to find the balance between speaking freely and speaking responsibly. The First Amendment guarantees freedom of speech to all U.S. citizens. At the same time, the government tries to set reasonable limits on this freedom to protect people from others' harmful expression.

Kids singing at a peace rally

Some citizens believe there should be no limits or laws restricting free speech. People should be completely free to say whatever they want, no matter whom they hurt or offend. Others believe the country's laws should be stricter. They argue that the

First Amendment was never meant to protect rude and **indecent** expression. They feel the government should prevent people from creating and distributing materials that are disgusting or offensive to the majority of U.S. citizens.

Some people have argued for a constitutional amendment making it illegal to burn the American flag. Others argue that flag burning is a form of expression protected by the First Amendment.

Some forms of expression that were once considered shocking—such as women wearing skirts above the ankle in the 1920s—are today considered acceptable.

Most Americans believe that some limits on free speech are a good idea. The trouble is that no two people agree completely on what is acceptable and what is not. Some things may seem funny to one person and hurtful to another. Also, society's standards have changed over time. Things that used to be thought shocking or indecent are now widely accepted. On the other hand, some things thought offensive today were considered perfectly acceptable years ago.

Should a recording artist be allowed to sing about illegal drug use? Should protesters be allowed to disrupt private businesses and disturb people's homes? Should public-school

What are the acceptable limits of free speech? Should students be allowed to pray before a public-school football game?

students be allowed to pray at football games or share their faith at school? If people dislike a particular program, should they simply turn the television off? Do we need more or fewer laws limiting free speech?

These questions are hard to answer, but Americans can debate these issues because they live in a country that respects and appreciates their right to freedom of speech.

To Find Out More

Here are some additional resources to help you learn more about freedom of speech:

 **Books**

Ditchfield, Christin. **Knowing Your Civil Rights.** Children's Press, 2004.

King, David C. **The Right to Speak Out.** Millbrook Press, 1997.

Quiri, Patricia Ryon. **The Bill of Rights.** Children's Press, 1999.

Sobel, Syl. **The U.S. Constitution and You.** Barron's Educational Series, Inc., 2001.

Steele, Philip. **Freedom of Speech.** Franklin Watts, 1997.

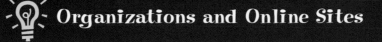

Organizations and Online Sites

Constitutional Rights Foundation

601 South Kingsley Drive
Los Angeles, CA 90005
http://www.crf-usa.org

This organization helps young people understand the value of the Constitution and the Bill of Rights.

U.S. National Archives & Records Administration

700 Pennsylvania Ave. NW
Washington, DC 20408
http://www.archives.gov

At this site you can view the Declaration of Independence, the U.S. Constitution, and the Bill of Rights.

The White House

1600 Pennsylvania Avenue NW
Washington, DC 20500
http://www.whitehousekids.gov

Check out the White House's site for kids for a virtual tour of the White House, as well as games, quizzes, time lines, and historical trivia.

Important Words

amendments changes made to a legal document

astronomer scientist who studies the stars and planets

criticize find fault in something

indecent not decent, moral, or proper

memorial something meant to help people remember someone or something

offensive unpleasant or upsetting

permit document giving one permission to do or own something

petitions letters signed by many people to demand change

political having to do with how the government is run

reputation general way a person is viewed

retraction written statement withdrawing or correcting an earlier remark

Index

(**Boldface** page numbers indicate illustrations.)

Meet the Author

Christin Ditchfield is an author and conference speaker, and is host of the nationally syndicated radio program *Take It to Heart!* Her articles have been featured in magazines all over the world. A former elementary-school teacher, Christin has written more than twenty-five books for children on a wide range of topics, including sports, science, and history. She makes her home in Sarasota, Florida.